Rays Of Hope

The Breaking Dawn of God's New Day

By Rev. Ken Wilcox

Cover Photo by Randy McDavid

Dedication

I would like to dedicate this small book to our wonderful community. This past year has indeed been a challenging time. I am grateful for all the support and hard work from our community to keep our beacon of hope and love illuminated. I am also very grateful to our board of trustees who have worked so hard along with all the other volunteers who have spent countless hours keeping our community together. I am very grateful to my friends, (particularly Delores Ellison who suggested this book), our wonderful neighbors and especially to my partner,

Tom, and our two furry children, who have kept me laughing and sane. A new day is coming and we have the power to make it into God's day of love, joy, community and goodness.

Introduction

When our board of trustees voted to close our building in March, we knew that we would have to change our mode of operation to keep ourselves viable during the crisis. Almost immediately we saw a need to create short affirmations to post on our social media. The affirmations you find in this book were those prayers. My hope is by collecting them for you in this small book they will continue to uplift and inspire. I know the Center for Spiritual Living in St. Augustine is a bright beacon of hope and inspiration for many. I pray that these affirmations can help you keep the high watch for yourself, your friends and family, for our community, our nation and the world. There is a breaking dawn of a new day for God's love, joy and laughter. It will be through our prayers and affirmations that we bring that better day to reality. It's within everyone of us to do and now is our day.

Spiritual Broadcasting

Today, God seeks to broadcast through me Its desires for greater love, joy, health, and prosperity. I have come to life so that God may experience the miracle of love through my eyes. I am here to know that I am a vital and necessary part of the unfoldment of Spirit's divine plan. God's plan for all of us is for us to know how loved and valued we are. We are on a mission from God to have as much laugher and joy in our lives as we can accept for ourselves. Today, I open my arms wide and allow the blessings of God to rain down upon me.

Living Joyfully

There is a way for us to move through life joyfully. Yes, there really is. If it were not true, then why would God have created us in the first place? To watch us toil through the troubles of the world? No, I believe we are here to sail through our lives on crystal blue waters guided by the gentle breeze of Spirit's love and compassion. We are loved by God. There is a way for us to make a joyful noise unto the Lord and it starts by our accepting the idea for ourselves. To know that we have a place in the heart of God. To know that the Power which set the universe into motion believes in us and has faith in our struggles. God has never doubted us for a moment, so why should we ever turn our eyes from the breaking dawn of God's possibilities. Today, let us hoist our sails to the blue skies of a new day and know that the gentle breeze of love guides us on in the adventure of life.

Life Gives

Life gives to me according to my faith. As I lift my eyes to my greater good, Spirit rains down blessings upon me. Today, I lift my eyes to greater love. I see myself surrounded by a loving family, fun friends and a welcoming community. Here now, I proclaim vibrant health for myself where I have the energy and ease to enjoy life. For these and even greater blessings, God only asks one thing of me: to release the wounds of the past and accept the blessings of the day. In faith, I move out into my world seeing and proclaiming the gifts of Spirit in all I meet.

Be You

No one can be you as well as you. God created you with all the little nooks and crannies of your personality so that Spirit's love could shine forth. It is in our broken places that the compassion of God breaks through into the reality of our lives. Today, I open my eyes to every God inspired idea so I can walk through the journey of my life with ease, peace and love.

Today is Your Day

The Good you are seeking is more powerful than any evil you have ever experienced. You have not come to life to be a victim, but a victor. You are here to be awed with how much God loves and supports you. God called you by name from star dust so that you could walk the soil of earth to breathe life into your dreams for greater health, more love and prosperity. Your life is not a problem to be solved, but a miracle unfolding. Today is your day to be the miracle God has called you to be.

Be the Light

Jesus said we are the light of the world. He also said that what he had done we could do even greater. Now is the time for us to get busy bringing about a greater good to our lives through the power of prayer. And the first good we need to accomplish is getting rid of the fear and turmoil dominating our lives. There is no power for evil in the universe. Evil only draws its strength from our misguided ideas. Fundamentally, evil comes from our misconception that we are not supported by God. That the good we seek is beyond our ability to attract it in our lives.

Today, see the good you are seeking as the light of Spirit showing up in your life through your love, joy and prosperity.

God is

God isn't just loving, God is love. God didn't just create life, God is life. So it is important for us to find a place of Universal Possibilities in our lives, and to use our affirmative prayers to allow those ideas to bloom into greater good for ourselves and our world. We are all a conduit for God's love and joy in our lives and in our world. What we are looking for we are looking with. Today, go be the blessing that God has called you to be. You did not come to life to be weak and wounded. You are here to be awed by the love and support of God for your dreams of health, love and prosperity. Today is your day and now is your time.

Channel of Love

Today, I am a channel of love. This love is the power and goodness of God made manifest in my life. The Creator and the created as one. Spirit knows itself by means of me, so today I know myself as loving, kind and compassionate. I choose to know myself as God knows me. Not as weak and wounded, but courageously compassionate. Today I step boldly into the Truth of myself.

Claim Your Miracle

You have a right to be here, and to live the best life possible. God did not call you by name from star dust to come to life to be a victim. You are here so that you can be awed by how much God loves and supports you. Supports your desires and dreams to live a life of health, love and prosperity. Right where you are, right as you are flows every idea you need to live the life of your greatest possibilities. You are here to live the life God prayed for you. You have never disappointed God. It is far more impressed with your possibilities than it has ever been disappointed with your mistakes. Your life is not a problem to be solved, but a miracle unfolding. Your job today is to claim your miracle, name your miracle and to make it your own.

Lifting Ourselves

How do we lift ourselves up when so much of the world seems to be spinning out of control? Early in the New Thought movement the focus was on right thinking. If we were clear in our own consciousness about the troubles we see around us, then the troubles we see would lose their power. In this time of change, we're being called to step out into the world. Not only to be conduits of thought but also avenues of action. We've not only been given a brain to direct but also hands and feet to bring about God's love and compassion. We are powerful beyond our wildest imaginations and now is the time. Do not be dismayed by the storm. What did Jesus ask of his disciples when they woke him in the midst of the storm: Have you no faith. We lift ourselves up as we lift others. We lift ourselves when we step out in faith and point toward the breaking dawn of hope and love.

Glory of God

We bring the spirit of God to our lives through our thinking. With a God of our understanding, goodness shines forth from our hearts and souls. We are not all of God, but all that we are is God. We are here to know that we are valued and needed. The unfoldment of God's great possibilities happens by means of our love, joy and health.Why are we going through this challenge? In order for something even greater to come about through our prayers and our good works. We are in life so God can awe us with the support and love it has to offer. Our challenge is to provide as many opportunities for God's love to flow into the world by means of us.

Be the Party

My teacher, Kennedy Shultz said that everyone had a good side. For some, it's the side we see coming. For others, it's the side we see going. Some people can make a party and some can ruin one. We have a choice on the energy we are allowing to flow into our lives and the energy we are allowing to vibrate from our hearts and soul.

Patterns of Love

All around us are patterns of Life and Love. The still, small voice of God forever encouraging us to be more and to love more. Closer to us than our next breath. From the mountaintop, to the valley, the desert and ocean it shouts at us from every direction. Yet, it can only become power to us when we proclaim ourselves as outlets of the love and joy of God made manifest.

Be Calm

There is a simple and effective way to pray. In fact, it's the exact way Jesus prayed. Deliberate and affirmative. Not begging and pleading. When we pray with faith why should we beg and plead? God does not need our pleads. God is waiting on us to announce our good so that it may rain down the blessings of heaven on our lives. Join Rev. Ken today with his talk: Be the Blessing. Many may ask, how can I be a blessing in this crisis when I barely can keep my head above water. Now is the time for us to rise up. In the darkest part of the night the candle can be seen the furthest. When the storm is howling the loudest is when the calm voice has the most authority. When Jesus was with his disciples in the boat and they came upon a storm the disciples gave into their fear. They woke Jesus up who had been asleep. Jesus asked them, "have you no faith?" The disciples had projected their fears in the future and had given up their power. Jesus had remained in the "Now" and had retained his authority. Like Jesus, now is the time for us to have the discipline not to give into our fears. Now is the time for us to retain our authority and to look out on the troubled waters of the

world and in faith declare,
"Be Calm."

The Good Within

There is great good within me. The Glory of God expresses itself in me and as me. The Divine and I are one. There is nothing too hard for God and there is nothing too good for me. Today, I let go of every thought of lack and limitation. Today, I choose to see myself as God sees me. I am not weak and wounded. I am strong and dynamic. Today, I walk with power. I walk with courage knowing that the goodness and glory of God flows through me, with me and for me.

At the center of our being is a pattern of goodness and perfection which has never been touched by our mistakes or confusion. That pattern is for a well lived life. A life of compassion, of joy and prosperity. God has never been confused about the life we deserve and now is the time for us to step into the life God has designed for us. There is nothing that we are facing or will ever face that we can't easily overcome with the right knowing of God's love. You plus God equals a majority in every situation. Today, is the day for us to see ourselves as God sees us, not as weak or wounded, but as magnificent and glorious.

Faith in God

Today, I rise up from any idea of lack or limitation. I choose to see myself as God sees me -- an answer to every problem in my life. God plus me equals a majority in every situation. So today, I will walk with courage and conviction. I am not weak and wounded. I am strong with the power of love and the truth of God's support. I am here in life to make a difference. To make the world a better place for my having been in it. God has faith in me and today I choose to place my faith in God.

Good at Hand

Today, I know that my good is at hand. With God's help, I lift my eyes to a better knowing for myself. A knowing of how to live with more love, joy and prosperity. I proclaim this right knowing for myself, and I look for this blessing in the lives of those around me. I am not in life to be weak or wounded. I am here to be a courageous witness for the compassion and love of God. A new heaven and a new earth is dawning. I see the rays of God's love breaking through the night of confusion and despair. Today, is the day I cast off the shackles of fear and doubt. Today is day the life

transforms from a problem
to be solved, to a miracle
unfolding.

One Power

I know that there is only one God, one Power, and that Power is perfect Love and Divine Intelligence. Here today, I know that love and wisdom flow into my life by means of me. Today, I open my thinking to the best inspirations God has for me to live with more love, joy and health. I am the beloved of Spirit and through me God pours It's greater possibilities into life. With these words I can move out into my world and be a blessing to myself and everyone in my life. Like the lighthouse that stands on the shore, my life can be a beacon of hope and love. Today, I cast open the widows of my thinking and allow the brilliance of Life's possibilities to shine forth.

The Arms of God

The Everlasting Arms. When we know that we are supported by the power and love of God we can rest with assurance that all is well in our lives. We have a power flowing through us that will allow us to heal whatever is in our past that needs to be healed, to deal with whatever challenge we will face in our future, and bless whatever it is before us to bless. We are not weak and wounded, but powerful beyond our greatest imaginations. We are here to make the world a better place for our having been in it. We do this by proclaiming the goodness in our lives and the blessings in the world. At the moment of our creation we were an answer to every problem we would ever confront. Spirit has never been discouraged or disappointed in us. It is far more impressed with our possibilities than our mistakes. Our job is to stay excited and prayerful for our God inspired dreams for they will light our way to a better and brighter day.

Victory Trumpets

There is but one God. One Power and one cause to all things. That power is perfect love. It is divine intelligence. It is flowing through me, with me and for me. It shows up in my life through my best ideas for myself. Ideas for more love, health, and compassion. Today, I lift my eyes up from the turmoil of the world. This confusion is not the truth of God, it is only the shadows of fear projecting into life. In my soul breaks a new dawn of my knowing of God's love. I have nothing to fear, for God is with me, urging me on to know something better for myself. Today, I walk out in the world secure in my knowing of God's love and support for me. The victory trumpets have sounded. The walls of fears and doubts are tumbling down, and the blessing of life is secure.

Freedom and Goodness

Our Divine Birthright is freedom and goodness. We have come to life to experience the joy of living. In fact, we are on a mission from Spirit to recognize and give gratitude for the glory of love and compassion. By recognizing and giving thanks for the love of God, we expand those blessings through our hearts and souls. We are in co-creation with Spirit to bring as much good as we can through our thoughts and prayers. Our prayers are needed and necessary. They are vital at this point in history. We are not waiting on God, God is waiting on us.

Star Dust

I've read that the majority
of the minerals in our bodies
don't originate here on
earth. They actually come
from star dust. Literally, we
are not of this world. This
may be where we do our
living, learning and work,
but it is not our home. We
are here so that we can
make the world a better
place for our having been in
it. We do that through our
partnership with Spirit. We
are on a mission from God
to have the best life
possible. To have so much
love and support in our lives
that we can become a joyful
giver to those around us.
Not in guilt and shame, but
with a heart of gladness we

birth a new heaven and a new earth.

We have come to life so that we can experience the love and support of God. We are here so that we can know for ourselves how much God is willing to awe us with Its kindness and compassion. While the world may be going through a challenge, God isn't. We walk the soil of this earth so that we can reflect through our lives the bright lights of God's possibilities.

Spirits Gifts

Today, I open my eyes to the goodness of God's love and compassion. I look for God's blessings and as I do my ability to see more of them increases. I proclaim the miracle of Spirit's gifts made manifest. I move out in the world with greater conviction of God's support and love. I know I am not weak or wounded. I have not come to life to be tested or judged. I am here to witness the joy of living through the support of God. Today, I lift my eyes from the troubles of the world and fix them on the support and encouragement that God flows to me and through me.

Create a Miracle

It is easier for us to create a miracle than we think. God is waiting on us to release that energy which set the universe into motion to bring about the joy of life. We are powerful beyond our greatest imagination. So here today, I release every idea and limitation that has ever held me back. I have created them, and I can let them go. Today, I will be about my Father's work and my Mother's compassion in creating a world of love and joy.

Glorious

In scripture it says that we are glorious in God's sight. We are pre-approved by God to be here and to have a good time. Jesus traveled all over Judea with 12 guys encouraging, inspiring and preforming miracles. Everyone knows when you get 12 young guys together one of them is going to tell a rude joke with sound effects. In other words, Jesus was having a good time helping bring about the blessings of Spirit. Through love, joy and laughter we can create a New Heaven and a New Earth. It is what we have been called to do. We have the power and Spirit has faith in us. God has never doubted us for a moment. God has always been more impressed with our potential than It has ever been angry over our mistakes. Isn't it time that we become more excited for our God inspired possibilities than we are worried about our human errors. Now is the time for us to step up to our power. To know we are glorious in the sight of God. To move out in the world strong with the love of God and courageous in Spirit's compassion. God is counting on us and we are up to the task.

Perfect Love

There is only one God and that God is perfect love and divine intelligence. That love and intelligence shows up in our lives through our best ideas. Joyful and loving ideas that remind us to lift our eyes from the turmoil and confusion of the world to the breaking dawn of God's possibilities. Ideas that make us feel more alive with the power and goodness of Spirit. Ideas that encourage us to step out in faith. To move out into our world courageous with God's compassion and bold with God's love.

My Path

Today I choose to see myself as God sees me. Not as weak or wounded, but glorious with the strength of God's love and compassion. This day I move out in my world knowing the goodness and support of Spirit is flowing through me. God places a lamp before my feet and makes my path clear. There is a song within my soul that wishes to sing to the glory of creation. Today, I release all fear and proclaim a new heaven and new earth through God's love and joy.

God possibilities.

Great possibilities

We bring the spirit of God to our lives through our thinking. With a God of our understanding, goodness shines forth from our hearts and souls. We are not all of God, but all that we are is God. We are here to know that we are valued and needed. The unfoldment of God's great possibilities happens by means of our love, joy and health.

Divine Ideas

Before you were anything, you were an idea in the mind of God. That which created the rings of Saturn, designed an orchid and designed the rear end of a gnat. Created you and approved of you. Has not been disappointed in you. Has not given up on you. Is seeking to help by giving you inspired ideas on how to have a more loving and joyful life because in doing that it will make the world a better place.

Lifting my eyes

Today, I lift my eyes up from the turmoil of the world. This confusion is not the truth of God, it is only the shadows of fear projecting into life. In my soul breaks a new dawn of my knowing of God's love. I have nothing to fear, for God is with me, urging me on to know something better for myself. Today, I walk out in the world secure in my knowing of God's love and support for me. The victory trumpets have sounded. The walls of fears and doubts are tumbling down and the blessing of life is secure.

Birthright

Our Divine Birthright is freedom and goodness. We have come to life to experience the joy of living. In fact, we are on a mission from Spirit to recognize and give gratitude for the glory of love and compassion. By recognizing and giving thanks for the love of God, we expand those blessings through our hearts and souls. We are in co-creation with Spirit to bring as much good as we can through our thoughts and prayers. Our prayers are needed and necessary. They are vital at this point in history. We are not waiting on God, God is waiting on us.

Life Gives

Life gives to me according to my faith. As I lift my eyes to my greater good, Spirit rains down blessings upon me. Today, I lift my eyes to greater love. I see myself surrounded by a loving family, fun friends and a welcoming community. Here now, I proclaim vibrant health for myself where I have the energy and ease to enjoy life. For these and even greater blessings, God only asks one thing of me: to release the wounds of the past and accept the blessings of the day. In faith, I move out into my world seeing and proclaiming the gifts of Spirit in all I meet.

Joyfully

There is a way for us to move through life joyfully. Yes, there really is. If it were not true, then why would God have created us in the first place? To watch us toil through the troubles of the world? No, I believe we are here to sail through our lives on crystal blue waters guided by the gentle breeze of Spirit's love and compassion. We are loved by God. There is a way for us to make a joyful noise unto the Lord and it starts by our accepting the idea for ourselves. To know that we have a place in the heart of God. To know that the Power which set the universe into motion believes in us and has faith in our struggles. God has never doubted us for a moment, so why should we ever turn our eyes from the breaking dawn of God's possibilities. Today, let us hoist our sails to the blue skies of a new day and know that the gentle breeze of love guides us on in the adventure of life.

Vital and Necessary

Today, God seeks to broadcast through me Its desires for greater love, joy, health, and prosperity. I have come to life so that God may experience the miracle of love through my eyes. I am here to know that I am a vital and necessary part of the unfoldment of Spirit's divine plan. God's plan for all of us is for us to know how loved and valued we are. We are on a mission from God to have as much laugher and joy in our lives as we can accept for ourselves. Today, I open my arms wide and allow the blessings of God to rain down upon me.

Knowing Ourselves

We have come to life so that we can experience the love and support of God. We are here so that we can know for ourselves how much God is willing to awe us with Its kindness and compassion. While the world may be going through a challenge, God isn't. We walk the soil of this earth so that we can reflect through our lives the bright lights of God's possibilities.

Your Truth

Today, know the truth for yourself, that there is only one God and that God is perfect love and divine intelligence. That love and intelligence shows up in our lives through our best ideas. Joyful and loving ideas that remind us to lift our eyes from the turmoil and confusion of the world to the breaking dawn of God's possibilities. Ideas that make us feel more alive with the power and goodness of Spirit. Ideas that encourage us to step out in faith. To move out into our world courageous with God's compassion and bold with God's love.

All Good

Good harmonizes my mind so that love can sing from my heart. Lifting my eyes from the confusion of this world I remind myself of the "all good" within my soul. That "all good" is the impulse for love that Spirit spoke into being by means of me. Today, I declare my unity with it. I let go of any idea of lack or limitations. Those ideas are but shadows of the truth and they flee this right knowing like the shadows fled the breaking dawn.

Fear Not

Did you know that, "Fear Not," is mentioned more times in scripture than any other admonition. Life is not for the faint hearted. We are going through a period in which we need to draw from our courage. It is helpful to remind ourselves that we are not alone. That power which created the universe is flowing through us, urging us on to know something better for ourselves. Urging us to be courageous in our compassion and bold with our love. Spirit has called you by name from star dust so that you can experience the goodness and joy of God by means of you. You were wonderfully made, and you are here on earth to do great and joyful work. God has never been discouraged about you for even a moment. It is far more excited about your possibilities than it has ever been disappointed over your mistakes. Today, is your day to release and let go of any fear holding you back. Our fears are only shadows of our own creation. They will disappear from our thinking as we lift our eyes to our God inspired possibilities.

Proclaim a Miracle

The turmoil of the world is but the shadows of our fears and worries. They have no power except that which we give them. The storm clouds may roil over our heads, but God's love is forever shining down upon us. Today, let us lift our eyes to a greater knowing. Let us look out on our world and proclaim God's goodness in the people we meet and the miracles we witness. Life is not a problem to be solved. Life is a miracle unfolding. This day, I proclaim myself a miracle. This day I move out into my world courageous with the love of God and bold with Spirit's compassion. Through

my love and joy God
proclaims a new heaven and
a new earth.

It's called a, "Prayer Practice," but that doesn't mean that it has to be painful or joyless. What does Scripture tells us: Make a joyful noise unto the Lord. If you are doing your prayers affirmatively you cannot help but feel better for having done them. Wouldn't you think that's a big hint from Spirit that we're doing them correctly. Helen Keller said that she believed every time a prayer was said some good happened in the world. Let us be an agent for good. Let us create a channel for the blessing of God to rain down upon humanity. We're just that powerful. We were created in the image and likeness of that which set the universe in motion. On this day let us use our prayers to bring about a new heaven and a new earth of love, joy, health, and prosperity. It is the world God had in mind when it spoke us into creation.

Greater Love

Dr. Holmes said we are afraid of our greatness because we are so tied to our littleness. We clutch the little anxiously and jealously, but so precariously to our hearts. It is essential to see beyond the little to that which is larger. None of us are perfect, so the challenge is to be great enough to rise to love, in charity and understanding and compassion.

The Spirit of God is calling upon us. We will never be satisfied with life until we answer that call. We will never be the person God has prayed for us to be until we step into our greater selves. In that place of faith, we will find ourselves to be in the vortex of miracles. It is within every one of us to do and now is the moment.

Please visit the Center for Spiritual Living, Saint Augustine

Online:
https://cslstaugustine.com

In person:
 1795 Old Moultrie Rd St Augustine Fl, 32084

Rev. Ken's Book: <u>Whispers of Heaven</u> is available online on Amazon.com

Made in the USA
Columbia, SC
13 October 2024

43505761R00040